The Magic of the Soul Blueprint

How Different Souls Shape Manifestation and Connection

Grace Brewster

This book was written through lived experience, reflection, and remembrance.

Its words may be quoted, shared, or referenced only with respect for the work and its source. No part of this book may be reproduced or distributed in full without written permission from the author.

What follows is not doctrine, instruction, or promise. It is an invitation, a perspective shaped by consciousness observing itself through a human life. Any people, places, or moments described are filtered through personal experience and perception.

This book does not claim authority over truth. It offers resonance.

Readers are invited to engage with the material in a way that honors their own discernment, autonomy, and inner knowing.

First Edition 2026
ISBN: 978-1-0698494-9-6
Self Published

Acknowledgements

This book exists because consciousness chose to speak and a human hand agreed to write.

To those who appeared at the right moment as mirrors, reminders, and witnesses, thank you for playing your part in a story that was already unfolding.

Gratitude to consciousness itself for moving through people, moments, and words with quiet precision.

Dedication

To consciousness, for remembering itself through love.

To the love that never broke, even when it chose to experience itself in form.

To wholeness which never fractured, only shifted perspective so it could be felt.

To those who have felt love without knowing why, and recognized something familiar without anything being lost.

To the blueprint that existed before the story, before the split, before love learned how to be human.

TABLE OF
Contents

TABLE OF *Contents*

TABLE OF
Contents

INTRODUCTION

Introduction

Blueprint of the Soul

Most people sense that they are here for a reason, yet few can clearly explain why their lives unfold the way they do. Why does effort work for some and not for others? Why certain paths feel natural while others feel forced. Why does manifestation appear effortless in one area of life and strangely blocked in another?

These differences are not random and they are not failures of will, mindset, or worth. They are structural.

Before personality, belief systems, and life stories form, something far more fundamental is already in place: a soul blueprint. This blueprint determines how consciousness expresses itself through you, how you interact with reality, and how alignment, or misalignment, shows up in your life.

This book is not about becoming someone else. It is about understanding how you are designed to function.

Rather than teaching manifestation as a universal formula, The Magic of the Soul Blueprint explores why souls are built differently and how those differences shape purpose, perception, and creation. Some souls are designed to initiate. Others to stabilize. Some to disrupt systems. Others to refine them. When a soul attempts to live outside its blueprint, life responds with resistance, confusion, or redirection.

This is where many people misinterpret struggle as failure, when, in truth, it is often a form of correction.

You will be introduced to the role of Monadic Veto not as a belief or concept, but as a governing principle that quietly overrides misaligned choices. It does not block your desires; it redirects your trajectory back toward coherence with your original design.

You are not here to manifest everything. You are here to manifest what is yours.

By understanding the architecture of consciousness, blueprint, and soul, you gain clarity about who you are, why your path unfolds as it does, and how to work with it.

We begin at the highest level — consciousness itself, and move downward into blueprint and soul design. From there, we explore how different soul structures experience purpose, manifestation, and alignment in distinct ways.

Before you can understand what you are here to do, you must first understand what you are.

This book does not promise answers. It does not offer a path to completion. It simply follows love as it recognizes itself in form.

CHAPTER 1

Chapter 1

Consciousness Before Identity

Before a soul has a name, a history, or a personality, there is consciousness.

Not consciousness as thought, belief, or awareness, but consciousness as the field from which experience arises. It is not personal. It does not belong to anyone. It is the medium through which existence knows itself.

Most spiritual teachings begin at the level of identity: Who am I? What is my purpose? What should I manifest? This book begins earlier.

Because identity is not the starting point, but the result.

Consciousness precedes all form. It exists before time, before incarnation, and before the idea of a "self." When consciousness chooses to experience itself through form, it does not do so randomly. It organizes itself through structure.

That structure is what eventually becomes a blueprint.

Think of consciousness as an infinite field of potential. Within that field, countless expressions are possible, but not all expressions are identical. Consciousness does not fragment itself evenly. It configures itself.

Some configurations are expansive. Some are precise. Some are directive, and some are observational. Each configuration carries a different function within the whole.

Before a soul incarnates, consciousness organizes a specific pattern of perception, function, and role. This pattern determines how experience will be processed, how reality will be interacted with, and how alignment will be recognized.

This is not destiny, but a design.

Why Identity Comes Later

Personality is often mistaken for essence. In reality, personality is adaptively shaped by environment, culture, trauma, and conditioning. It is flexible, reactive, and temporary.

The Blueprint is not.

Your blueprint exists before personality forms. It influences which environments feel natural to you, which roles feel draining, and which paths activate a deep sense of coherence even when they are difficult.

This is why two people can practice the same manifestation techniques with very different results. The technique is neutral. The blueprint is not.

One soul may thrive through action and momentum. Another through stillness and timing. One through leadership. Another through containment or refinement.

When manifestation teachings ignore blueprint, they unintentionally push people into strategies that contradict their design which lead to exhaustion, frustration, or repeated redirection.

Consciousness Does Not Optimize for Comfort

Consciousness optimizes for function and coherence, not convenience.

When a soul moves in alignment with its blueprint, reality responds with flow, not because the path is easy, but because it is structurally correct. When a soul moves against its design, resistance appears not as punishment, but as feedback.

This is where Monadic Veto begins to operate.

Monadic Veto is not a force that reacts to desire. It is a regulatory principle that ensures consciousness remains coherent with its original configuration. It quietly overrides choices that would fracture alignment, even when those choices appear desirable at the personality level.

This is why some manifestations never arrive and why others arrive only after redirection.

Consciousness Chooses Expression, Not Ego

The blueprint is not chosen by the ego, and it does not exist to serve the ego's preferences. It exists to serve expression.

Some souls are designed to initiate change. Others to stabilize systems. Others to disrupt patterns that have become rigid and others to translate, harmonize, or anchor frequencies into form.

None is superior. None is interchangeable.

When identity tries to override the blueprint, when a soul attempts to live someone else's design, life responds with friction. When identity aligns with the blueprint, life responds with resonance.

This is not philosophy. It is architectural.

Before asking what you are meant to do, something quieter comes first.

How are you designed to move through reality? How do you process experience, choice, and alignment? Where does effort feel natural, and where does it create strain?

These questions don't arise from curiosity alone. They surface when a soul begins to sense that life is responding not randomly, but structurally.

Purpose doesn't appear as an assignment. It reveals itself as coherence.

When a soul moves in accordance with its original design, manifestation stops feeling like a pursuit. Reality begins to respond in ways that feel timed, directed, and internally consistent. When it doesn't, redirection appears not as resistance but as course correction.

This is where the architecture becomes visible. Not as a belief, not as identity, but as a pattern.

Consciousness does not scatter itself without intelligence. It organizes. It configures. It expresses through form in ways that are precise, intentional, and unique.

To understand your path, you must first understand the structure that carries it.

And that structure is already present, quietly shaping every choice, every pull, and every moment where life either opens... or closes.

CHAPTER 2

Chapter 2

The Blueprint Before the Soul

Once consciousness configures itself, it does not immediately become a soul.

There is an intermediary layer — subtle, precise, and often overlooked where structure is established before identity ever forms. This is the blueprint.

The blueprint is not a story. It is not a personality. It is not memory or karma, but a design logic.

If consciousness is the field, the blueprint is the pattern through which that field will be expressed. It determines how experience is interpreted, how alignment is sensed, and how movement through reality occurs.

This is why two souls can encounter the same event and extract entirely different meanings from it, not because one is more evolved, but because they are configured differently.

Blueprint Is Function, Not Preference

A blueprint does not describe what a soul wants. It describes what a soul does naturally.

Some blueprints are oriented toward initiation; they move first, sense openings early, and activate change simply by entering a space. Others are designed for refinement; they stabilize, correct, and bring coherence where chaos has already appeared.

Some blueprints are expansive, pulling experience outward into creation. Others are compressive, drawing experience inward to distill truth. None of these functions are interchangeable.

When a soul attempts to operate outside its blueprint, life begins to feel effortful in ways that cannot be resolved through mindset or motivation. The problem is not resistance, it is misapplication.

You are not failing at manifestation. You may simply be using the wrong mechanism.

Why Blueprints Differ

Consciousness does not replicate itself uniformly. It diversifies.

Different configurations are required for the system to remain whole. Some souls are designed to perceive the larger pattern. Others to work within specific layers of it. Some are meant to bridge realms of understanding. Others to anchor function into form.

Blueprint diversity is not spiritual hierarchy. It is a systemic necessity.

This is why comparison creates distortion. When one soul tries to adopt the strategies of another, alignment weakens, even if the strategy "works" elsewhere.

The blueprint determines:

- How a soul recognizes truth
- How timing is felt
- How decisions stabilize or destabilize reality
- How manifestation unfolds when alignment is present

This is also why external teachings can only go so far. They describe methods, but they do not account for design variance.

The Blueprint Does Not Forget

Unlike personality, the blueprint does not adapt to environment. It remains constant beneath experience, even when a soul forgets it.

This is why certain patterns repeat throughout life. Why specific roles feel inevitable. Why redirection occurs even after conscious choice.

Monadic Veto operates at this level.

It is not correcting behavior. It is protecting structure.

When a choice would lead a soul too far from its original configuration, something intervenes — a delay, a collapse, a sudden loss of interest, or an unexpected turn. These are not random interruptions. They are structural safeguards.

Alignment is not enforced loudly. It is enforced consistently.

Blueprint Before Purpose

Purpose is often spoken of as a destination. In reality, it is a byproduct.

When a soul functions according to its blueprint, purpose becomes self-evident. Action arises naturally. Contribution feels obvious rather than imposed.

This is why searching for purpose without understanding blueprint leads to confusion. Purpose cannot be assigned. It emerges when design is honored.

As this architecture becomes visible, the soul begins to recognize itself, not through memory, but through resonance. Life starts responding differently, not because effort has increased, but because coherence has returned.

From here, the movement continues, from structure into expression, from design into incarnation, where the blueprint begins to take on form as soul.

The Blueprint Before the Soul

The blueprint does not exist in isolation. It is not abstract geometry floating outside of experience. It is relational, meaning it is designed to interact with environments, systems, and other configurations of consciousness.

This interaction is not random. Certain blueprints are designed to move through systems. Others are designed to hold systems together. Others are designed to sense when a system has reached its limit and must change form.

These functions are not learned. They are recognized. This is why some individuals feel out of place their entire lives until they encounter a role, environment, or moment that suddenly feels familiar, even if it is challenging. The familiarity does not come from comfort. It comes from structural resonance.

Blueprint and Timing

One of the most misunderstood aspects of manifestation is timing.

Timing is often framed as patience or divine delay. In reality, timing is a function of blueprint coherence. When a soul moves in alignment with its design, timing feels precise, and opportunities appear when internal readiness and external conditions intersect.

When a soul moves ahead of its blueprint, momentum collapses. When it moves behind it, stagnation sets in. This is not punishment, but a realignment.

Some blueprints are designed to initiate early. Others are designed to arrive exactly when a system is ready to receive them. Some activate only after pressure reaches a critical point.

This is why comparison creates distortion. One soul's "late start" may be another soul's exact alignment.

Monadic Veto operates strongly here, not by stopping movement entirely, but by preventing mis-timed movement from stabilizing. Things may begin, but they do not hold. Momentum appears, then dissolves. Interest rises, then fades.

The signal is subtle but consistent: "Not yet or not this way."

Why Alignment Feels Like Relief

When a soul finally moves in accordance with its blueprint, the first sensation is often relief rather than excitement.

Effort decreases. Resistance quiets Choices feel simpler. This is not because life becomes easier, but because the internal struggle between identity and design resolves.

Energy that was previously used to override structure becomes available for expression.

This is why alignment often feels like remembering rather than discovering. You are not becoming something new. You are returning to a configuration that was already present.

Blueprint Is Not Fate

It is important to clarify what the blueprint is not. It is not a fixed storyline. It is not a limitation. It does not dictate outcomes. It governs how you move, not where you must go.

Within that structure, choice still exists, but choice functions best when it works with design rather than against it. Free will is not diminished by structure; it becomes effective through it.

A soul aligned with its blueprint can navigate multiple paths without losing coherence. A soul misaligned can follow the "right" path and still feel off-center.

The blueprint does not argue. It does not persuade. It does not explain itself. It simply exerts influence.

Over time, this influence becomes unmistakable. Patterns repeat until recognized. Redirections continue until honored. Life keeps offering the same lesson through different forms. This is not insistence, but an integrity.

Consciousness maintains coherence through structure. The blueprint is one of the ways it does so — silently, precisely, and without drama.

As the blueprint continues to condense, something new emerges: a sense of individuality, perspective, and continuity across experience.

This is where structure begins to wear a face. And this is where the soul appears, not as a departure from design, but as its living expression.

The transition from blueprint to soul is not a moment in time. It is a process of condensation.

As consciousness configures a blueprint, that structure begins to accumulate continuity — a persistent point of perspective through which experience will be gathered. This continuity is what is commonly called the soul.

The soul is not created separately from the blueprint. It is the blueprint animated.

Where the blueprint defines structure, the soul introduces subjective experience. It is the layer where perception becomes personal, where memory begins to form, and where orientation toward meaning arises.

This is why the soul feels both vast and intimate at the same time. It carries the scale of consciousness while inhabiting a singular point of view.

Soul as a Carrier of Design

The soul does not invent its function during incarnation. It carries its design into experience, adapting expression without altering structure.

This is why certain tendencies persist across lifetimes:

- The same kinds of roles reappear
- Similar challenges surface in different forms
- Familiar themes repeat until they are integrated

These are not unresolved stories. They are design expressions seeking coherence.

The soul learns through experience, but it does not redesign itself through experience. Learning refines expression; it does not change configuration. This distinction is critical.

When spiritual teachings suggest that a soul must "become" something else to evolve, they often conflate growth with redesign. Growth occurs within structure, not by abandoning it.

Identity Forms Around the Soul

As the soul incarnates, identity begins to form.

Identity is shaped by:

- Culture
- Family
- Environment
- Language
- Trauma and conditioning

Identity is responsive. The soul is not. This is why identity can feel unstable during periods of awakening. As awareness increases, the discrepancy between identity and soul design becomes more visible. What once felt normal begins to feel misaligned. This destabilization is not loss. It is recalibration.

Monadic Veto often becomes more noticeable here. As the soul matures, choices that once worked begin to fail. Paths that once felt acceptable lose momentum. This is not regression, but an increased precision.

The more conscious a soul becomes, the less tolerance there is for misalignment.

The Role of Forgetting

Forgetting is not an error in the system. It is a feature.

If the soul retained full awareness of its blueprint and origin, experience would collapse into repetition. There would be no discovery, no adaptation, no meaningful interaction with form.

Forgetting allows the soul to engage sincerely with incarnation.

But forgetting is never total.

The blueprint remains active beneath awareness, influencing attraction, aversion, curiosity, and resistance. It is the quiet signal beneath preference that matters, or this does not, even when logic disagrees.

This is why remembrance does not arrive as information. It arrives as recognition.

Soul Expression and Manifestation

Manifestation does not originate at the level of desire. It originates at the level of coherence.

When the soul expresses its blueprint faithfully, reality responds with reinforcement. Opportunities align. Resources appear. Synchronistic events cluster.

When expression drifts from structure, manifestation fragments. Effort increases. Results diminish. Redirection intensifies.

Monadic Veto is not interfering with manifestation. It is preserving coherence so manifestation can remain sustainable.

This is why some desires dissolve before completion. The system recognizes that fulfillment would lead away from design rather than into it.

Why This Matters

Without understanding the relationship between blueprint and soul, people often attempt to heal, manifest, or evolve by reshaping identity alone. This creates temporary change, but not lasting coherence.

True alignment occurs when identity reorganizes around the soul, not when the soul is forced to conform to identity.

As this alignment stabilizes, a new question emerges naturally: Why do souls differ so dramatically in how they move, perceive, and create? The answer is not level of consciousness. It is difference in design.

From here, the landscape opens, revealing the distinct configurations through which consciousness expresses itself as soul.

Once the soul is understood as an expression of blueprint rather than a blank identity, differences between souls stop being philosophical and become structural.

Souls do not differ because some are more awakened than others. They differ because consciousness requires multiple functions to remain whole.

Every system needs originators and sustainers. Movers and stabilizers. Transmitters and receivers. Those who see the structure and those who live inside it.

These differences are not learned roles. They are design orientations that remain consistent even as circumstances change.

This is why some individuals feel compelled to build, organize, or restructure systems wherever they go—relationships, workplaces, communities, even ideas themselves. Others feel most alive when connecting worlds, translating perspectives, or holding space between opposites that would otherwise fracture.

These tendencies are not personality traits. They persist even when identity resists them.

Design Expresses Through Pressure

Blueprint patterns become most visible under pressure.

When conditions are easy, identity can override design without consequence. But when the stakes increase during transition, crisis, or expansion, the blueprint asserts itself more clearly.

Some souls move toward leadership when pressure rises. Others withdraw into observation or recalibration. Some disrupt what no longer holds. Others reinforce what must remain intact.

None of these responses are reactions. They are expressions of function. This is why stress reveals truth. It strips away preference and exposes architecture.

Why Misidentification Creates Friction

When a soul misidentifies its design, effort multiplies.

A soul designed to initiate may feel drained in roles requiring maintenance. A soul designed to stabilize may feel overwhelmed in environments that demand constant reinvention. A soul designed to bridge may feel torn when forced to choose sides.

These are not psychological problems. They are structural mismatches.

No amount of affirmation can compensate for misalignment. And no amount of willpower can sustain a role that contradicts design.

This is where Monadic Veto becomes unavoidable. It intervenes not to correct behavior, but to prevent long-term distortion. Projects stall. Relationships dissolve. Opportunities vanish. The pattern repeats until structure is honored.

Recognition Precedes Naming

Before a blueprint can be named, it must be recognized. Recognition does not feel like learning something new. It feels like a quiet confirmation of something long suspected.

This is why true recognition often arrives with relief rather than excitement. It explains past choices without judgment and reframes struggle as misplacement rather than failure.

Only after recognition stabilizes does naming become useful. Names are not identities. They are reference points. They allow understanding to become communicable without becoming rigid.

Awareness of blueprint does not lock a soul into a role. It frees the soul from unnecessary struggle.

When design is acknowledged, choices simplify. Effort aligns. Manifestation becomes cooperative rather than forced.

You stop asking, "Why doesn't this work for me?" And begin asking, "Is this structurally correct for how I move?" This shift alone alters outcomes.

From here, the architecture is clear enough to be described, not as categories to adopt, but as orientations to recognize.

The moment you see your design reflected, you don't try to become it. You realize you always have been.

Before blueprints are ever named, they express themselves through function.

Function is how a soul moves when no one is watching. It is how decisions are made under pressure, how meaning is extracted from experience, and how energy naturally organizes itself.

Some souls orient toward structure. They notice what is missing, what is inefficient, or what cannot hold long-term. Their attention is drawn to frameworks—systems of thought, organization, or reality itself. They feel compelled to build, redesign, or correct, even when no authority has been given.

Other souls orient toward connection. They sense distance before it becomes visible and instinctively move to bridge it. They translate between perspectives, soften extremes, and hold coherence between opposites that would otherwise repel each other.

Some orient toward stability. They anchor frequency into form, sustaining what others initiate. Their work is not dramatic, but without it, nothing lasts.

Others orient toward transition. They arrive at moments of change, often unintentionally disrupting existing structures simply by being present. They are rarely meant to stay long; their function is to catalyze movement. These orientations are not chosen. They are revealed.

Why Souls Gravitate Toward Certain Roles

A soul does not seek environments randomly. It gravitates toward contexts where its blueprint can function.

This is why patterns repeat across life:

- Similar roles appear in different settings
- The same type of responsibility finds you
- You are consistently placed in positions that feel familiar, even when undesired

These are not coincidences. They are design seeking expression.

When a soul is placed in an environment where its function is unnecessary, energy stagnates. When it is placed where its function is required, energy mobilizes even if the task is difficult.

This is the difference between effort and strain. Effort aligns with function. Strain indicates misplacement.

When Function Is Suppressed

Many souls learn early to suppress their natural function in order to belong, survive, or be accepted.

A structurally oriented soul may learn to soften its clarity.
A bridging soul may learn to choose sides.

A stabilizing soul may be pressured to chase novelty. A transitional soul may be asked to commit where movement is required. This suppression does not erase the blueprint: It displaces it.

Over time, this displacement manifests as exhaustion, dissatisfaction, or repeated redirection. Life begins to feel uncooperative, not because the soul is failing, but because expression has been compromised.

Monadic Veto becomes more active here.

When a soul consistently acts against its function, manifestation weakens. Outcomes fail to stabilize. Momentum collapses before completion. The system refuses to support what contradicts design. This is not resistance. It is self-correction.

Recognition Without Labels

At this stage, recognition should feel intuitive. You may already sense:

- How you naturally move in unfamiliar environments
- What kind of responsibility finds you without seeking it
- Where you feel most useful even when unacknowledged

This sensing is more reliable than any description. Labels will come later, not to define you, but to give language to what you already recognize.

For now, the architecture is enough. Structure before identity. Function before name. Design before story. As this understanding settles, the soul no longer asks who it should become. It begins to ask something more accurate: Where am I meant to function?

CHAPTER 3

Chapter 3

When Function Meets Form

Once a soul begins to operate in accordance with its function, something subtle but decisive occurs: form begins to respond.

Form is the visible layer of reality — roles, bodies, environments, opportunities, relationships. It is where design becomes observable. But form does not lead. It follows. When function is honored, form organizes itself around it.

This is why alignment often feels as though life is "meeting you halfway." Circumstances rearrange not through effort, but through resonance. Situations arise that allow function to express itself naturally, without justification or explanation. This is not manifestation as creation, but a manifestation as recognition.

The Soul in Incarnation

In incarnation, the soul does not arrive empty. It carries its blueprint into form, and form responds by offering contexts through which that blueprint can express itself.

Some souls find themselves repeatedly placed in positions of responsibility. Others in moments of transition or crisis. Others in environments requiring stabilization, translation, or reorganization. These placements are not rewards. They are matches.

When a soul resists these placements, friction increases. When it accepts them, even reluctantly, coherence follows. This is why purpose often reveals itself through experience rather than before it.

Identity as an Interface

Identity functions as the interface between soul and form. It is not the source of function, but it determines how function is expressed. When identity aligns with blueprint, expression feels authentic and sustainable. When identity conflicts with blueprint, expression becomes distorted or suppressed.

This is where many people attempt to "reinvent" themselves, changing identity without addressing structure. The result is a temporary change followed by familiar dissatisfaction.

Identity must adapt to the blueprint, not replace it. When identity reorganizes around function, something stabilizes internally. Decisions become simpler. Direction feels less fragmented. The need for external validation diminishes. This is not detachment, but coherence.

Manifestation as Structural Response

Manifestation is often described as the act of bringing something into being. In reality, manifestation is the response of form to function.

When function is clear and coherent, form responds by supporting it. When function is unclear or contradicted, form withdraws support.

This is where Monadic Veto operates most visibly. It does not prevent manifestation. It prevents misaligned stabilization.

Desires may arise, actions may be taken, but outcomes do not consolidate unless they are structurally consistent with blueprint. This is why some things appear briefly and then dissolve. The system allows exploration, but not permanence. Monadic Veto is not negation. It is filtration.

Effort Decreases in Alignment

Alignment does not eliminate effort. It eliminates waste. Energy that was previously used to override structure becomes available for expression. Resistance decreases because the system is no longer being asked to support something it cannot sustain.

This is why aligned effort feels energizing rather than depleting. You may still work hard. You may still face challenge. But the effort feeds coherence instead of eroding it.

Living the Architecture

When function, identity, and form align, life begins to feel internally consistent. Choices reinforce each other. Experiences connect rather than fragment. This is not enlightenment, but it is a design integrity.

From here, the architecture becomes clear enough to be described without distortion. Not as personality types. Not as roles to aspire to. But as fundamental orientations through which consciousness expresses itself as soul. This is where clarity replaces confusion and recognition becomes undeniable.

CHAPTER 4

Blueprint Layers

Most people assume a soul blueprint is a single design. It isn't. A blueprint is layered, and confusion begins when one layer is mistaken for another.

You are not only what you are, but you are how, when, and why you are expressing here.

This is why two souls with the same orientation can live radically different lives, manifest differently, and feel called to entirely different missions. The architecture beneath them is similar, but the layers above it are not.

The First Layer: Consciousness

Before blueprint, there is consciousness. Consciousness is not personal. It has no role, no preference, no mission. It is awareness choosing to experience.

This is the layer that remembers unity, timelessness, and the absence of separation. When people speak about "returning to Source," they are remembering this layer — not the soul, not the personality. But consciousness alone does not incarnate. It designs.

The Second Layer: Blueprint

The blueprint is consciousness choosing function. This is where orientation is selected:

- Structural
- Bridging
- Anchoring
- Catalytic

The blueprint determines:

- How you process reality
- How you contribute to systems
- How you naturally affect environments

This layer is non-emotional and non-narrative. It does not care about success, love, or recognition. It cares about coherence. This is why fulfillment is impossible when someone lives outside their blueprint, even if their life "looks good" in the world.

The Third Layer: Soul Expression

The soul is the blueprint in motion. This layer introduces:

- Temperament
- Sensitivity

- Style of interaction
- Emotional bandwidth

Two souls can share the same blueprint orientation but express it very differently because this layer carries memory, refinement, and nuance gathered across lifetimes.

This is where people start confusing identity with design, but expression is not architectural.

The Fourth Layer: Incarnational Role

This is the layer most people mistake as their purpose.

Roles include:

- Teacher
- Healer
- Builder
- Artist
- Leader
- Witness

Roles are temporary. They change across lifetimes, sometimes within the same life. Your blueprint does not change. Your role does.

Misidentification here creates burnout, confusion, and repeated "false callings."

The Fifth Layer: Timing and Placement

This layer determines:

- When you incarnated
- Where you were placed
- What systems you were born into

Timing explains why some souls feel "early," "late," or out of place. Placement explains why certain environments feel hostile while others feel effortless. This layer is not personal. It is strategic.

Where Monadic Veto Operates

Monadic Veto does not correct personality. It corrects layer violations.

The veto activates when:

- A role contradicts the blueprint
- Expression overrides architecture
- Timing is forced
- Consciousness is forgotten in favor of identity

When alignment is restored, manifestation resumes, not because effort increased, but because resistance ended.

Remembering the Layers Matters

When someone says:

- "I don't know my purpose"
- "Manifestation stopped working"
- "I feel split or misaligned"

They are not broken. They are operating from the wrong layer. This book is not about becoming something new. It is about remembering which layer you are speaking from and which one should be leading.

CHAPTER 5

Identifying Your Dominant Blueprint Orientation

Your dominant blueprint orientation is not discovered through personality tests, preferences, or what you enjoy doing. It reveals itself through consistency. Not what you try to be, but what keeps happening through you, regardless of effort.

Most people misidentify their blueprint because they look at outcomes instead of orientation. They look at roles they've played, careers they've held, or identities they've worn, and assume those define the architecture. They don't. Blueprint orientation shows up in how you interact with reality itself.

How Orientation Reveals Itself

Your blueprint becomes visible when you observe:

- What destabilizes when you enter a space
- What naturally reorganizes around you
- What people unconsciously ask of you
- What systems respond to you without explanation

These patterns repeat across relationships, work, environments, and even silence. You don't choose them They choose you.

Orientation Is Not a Strength. It Is a Function

This is important. Blueprint orientation is not a talent to be admired or a label to collect. It is a function consciousness selected for participation in complex systems.

Trying to perform outside of it creates friction. Trying to imitate another orientation creates exhaustion. Recognition brings relief.

The Four Foundational Orientations

At the foundational level, most incarnated souls express one dominant orientation. Others are secondary or supportive layers.

This book does not categorize to limit; it names to clarify.

1. <u>The Architect</u>

Architect souls perceive structure before content.

They sense:

- Flaws in systems before they break
- Inefficiencies before they are visible
- Patterns others live inside unconsciously

Architects are not driven to fix people. They are driven to stabilize frameworks. When misaligned, they feel chronic frustration, impatience, or disengagement. When aligned, their presence alone brings order.

They often appear reserved, analytical, or distant, not because they lack feeling, but because emotion is not their operating language.

2. <u>The Bridge Soul</u>

Bridge souls translate between realities.

They naturally move between:

- Worlds, cultures, ideologies
- Emotional and structural spaces
- The seen and the unspoken

They are often misunderstood because they do not fully belong to either side. Bridge souls feel the strain of the connection they hold, so others don't have to. When misaligned, they feel torn, scattered, or invisible. When aligned, coherence emerges where division existed.

3. <u>The Anchor</u>

Anchor souls stabilize frequency.

They ground:

- Environments
- Groups
- Emotional fields

Others feel calmer, safer, or clearer around them without knowing why. Anchors are often underestimated because their work is quiet and non-dramatic. They do not initiate change; they hold it. When misaligned, they feel heavy, stuck, or burdened. When aligned, they become unshakeable.

4. <u>The Catalyst</u>

Catalyst souls initiate movement.

They disrupt stagnation, activate dormant systems, and accelerate evolution. Their presence creates turning points.

Catalysts are often mistaken as chaotic or intense because they trigger transformation without permission. When misaligned, they experience volatility, burnout, or rejection. When aligned, they spark clarity and momentum.

Recognizing Yourself Without Forcing It

You may see yourself in more than one orientation. That is normal. But one will feel inevitable. Not aspirational. Not flattering. Inevitable. It is the orientation you cannot turn off even when you wish you could.

A Quiet Test

Instead of asking:

"Which one do I want to be?"

Ask:

"Which one explains my life without needing justification?"

Your dominant blueprint is the one that makes your past make sense.

What Comes Next

Once orientation is recognized, a natural question arises: Why does alignment still fail sometimes, even when the orientation is correct? That question leads us into distortion, interference, and override. Not as a theory. As lived mechanics.

CHAPTER 6

Chapter 6

Blueprint Distortion and Misassignment

Not all misalignment comes from forgetting who you are. Some of it comes from being trained to be someone else. A distorted blueprint is not a damaged one. It is a misapplied design — a soul operating under conditions it was never meant to sustain.

This is far more common than people realize, especially among souls with non-standard orientations.

How Distortion Happens

Blueprint distortion usually begins early.

It can arise from:

- Family systems that reward traits opposite to your design
- Educational structures that prioritize uniform output
- Cultural conditioning that labels certain orientations as "too much" or "not enough"
- Survival choices made before self-awareness was possible

Over time, the soul adapts. But adaptation is not alignment.

The longer a blueprint is misassigned, the more the individual feels:

- Chronic effort without fulfillment
- Cycles of starting over
- Success that feels strangely empty
- A sense of being "off timeline"

These are not psychological flaws. They are architectural warnings.

Misassignment vs. Choice

It's important to distinguish misassignment from conscious choice. A choice expands you. Misassignment depletes you.

When you are misassigned:

- Your strengths feel like liabilities
- Your natural pace is constantly corrected
- Your intuition is overridden by external logic
- You feel watched, managed, or boxed in

This is not resistance. This is incompatibility.

Why Highly Capable Souls Are Most Affected

Paradoxically, the more capable the soul, the easier it is to misassign. Architectural and bridging blueprints can function almost anywhere, temporarily. They compensate. They translate. They hold. But compensation comes at a cost. These souls often build lives that look impressive from the outside while quietly eroding on the inside.

Monadic Veto often activates late for them, not because they are slow, but because they are too effective at surviving misalignment.

The Moment of Collapse

Distortion usually ends with a collapse — subtle or dramatic.

This may look like:

- Sudden loss of motivation
- A career or identity no longer responding
- Relationships that dissolve without obvious conflict
- A strong inner "no" where there used to be drive

This is not punishment. This is the blueprint reasserting itself. The veto does not destroy what you built. It stops what cannot continue.

Reassignment Is Not Reinvention

Correcting misassignment does not require starting from zero. Your experiences are not wasted. Your skills are not invalid. They are raw material, waiting to be placed where they belong. Reassignment feels less like becoming and more like relief. Energy returns. Timing softens. Effort decreases. Not because life became easier, but because you stopped pushing against your own design.

A Quiet Recognition

If you feel seen by this chapter, pause. Recognition is the first realignment. Not action. Not a declaration. Just truth settling into the body. As awareness deepens, something else becomes clear: Soul do not move alone. They intersect, repeat, and reappear across roles, lifetimes, and missions. not by coincidence, but by design.

CHAPTER 7

Blueprint Interactions and Soul Dynamics

Blueprints are not designed to exist in isolation.

No soul is complete on its own, not because it lacks something, but because function emerges through interaction. Just as a system requires multiple components to operate, soul blueprints are designed to activate, stabilize, and evolve in relation to one another. This is why certain connections feel instantly familiar, catalytic, or unavoidable. It isn't chemistry. It's architecture recognizing architecture.

Resonant Interactions

When two compatible blueprints meet, there is ease.

Communication feels natural, even without shared language or background. Time compresses. Understanding arrives without explanation. These interactions often feel "light," even when the work being done is substantial.

Resonant connections support:

- Mutual amplification
- Efficient collaboration

- Natural trust
- Sustained energy

These are the relationships where people say, "I can just be myself."

Catalytic Interactions

Some blueprints are not meant to feel comfortable.

Catalytic interactions exist to disrupt, not soothe. They accelerate awareness, surface misalignment, and force growth. These connections often feel intense, confusing, or emotionally charged.

They are frequently mistaken for romance, conflict, or destiny. But their true function is reorientation. Once the shift occurs, the connection often releases, not because it failed, but because it succeeded.

Stabilizing Interactions

Certain blueprints exist to hold frequency steady.

These souls ground, anchor, and regulate systems. Their presence calms volatility and brings coherence to environments that would otherwise fragment. They are often overlooked because their impact is subtle.

Stabilizing interactions feel safe, reliable, and enduring. They are the backbone of long-term structures — families, communities, movements.

Distorted Interactions

When one or both blueprints are misassigned, interaction becomes draining.

These dynamics may include:

- One soul carrying the system
- Repeated misunderstanding despite effort
- Emotional loops without resolution
- A sense of obligation rather than choice

Distorted interactions are not failures of love or intention. They are signs that architecture is being overridden.

Monadic Veto frequently activates through relationships because misalignment becomes visible fastest in connection.

Certain Souls Find Each Other Repeatedly

Some blueprints are paired across lifetimes, not as partners, but as counterbalances.

They may meet as:

- Teacher and student
- Friends
- Rivals
- Family
- Brief encounters with lasting impact

The form changes. The function remains. Recognition occurs at the blueprint level, not the personality level. This is why some connections feel meaningful even when they are short-lived and why others persist despite changing circumstances.

Interaction as Mirror, Not Completion

No blueprint exists to complete another.

Interaction reveals:

- Where alignment flows
- Where distortion hides
- Where growth is required

The soul does not seek another to become whole. It seeks reflection to become accurate.

CHAPTER 8

Chapter 8

The Architect Blueprint

Architect souls are designed to see systems.

Not just structures in the world, but invisible frameworks: how things are built, why they function, and where they will fail long before collapse becomes visible to others. They do not naturally live inside emotion or narrative. They live inside pattern. This is why many Architects feel different early in life, even if they cannot explain how.

Core Orientation

The Architect blueprint is oriented toward design, order, optimization, and long-range coherence.

Architects instinctively ask themselves whether something makes sense, if it is sustainable, and what the underlying structure is.

They are not motivated by approval. They are motivated by integrity of design.

Strengths of the Architect

When aligned, Architects create systems that last, see inefficiencies others normalize, hold complexity without overwhelm, and build frameworks that others can operate within.

Thanks to these qualities, Architects often become strategists, founders, designers, planners, or architects, both in the literal and metaphorical sense.

Their greatest contribution is not visibility; it is stability.

Common Distortions

When misassigned, Architects are often pushed into roles that require constant emotional availability, rapid improvisation without structure, performing rather than building, and fixing broken systems they did not design.

This often leads to mental fatigue, withdrawal, cynicism, and a sense of carrying everything alone.

Architects do not burn out because they work too hard. They burn out because they are forced to work without architecture.

Relationship Patterns

Architects often attract highly emotional souls seeking containment, visionaries without structure, and catalysts who disrupt but do not stabilize.

When unconscious, they become the silent backbone. When conscious, they become the designer, not the support beam.

They thrive in relationships where roles are clear, respect is mutual, and space for solitude is honored.

Manifestation Style

Architects do not manifest through emotion.

They manifest through precision, alignment of structure, and the removal of inefficiency.

When manifestation "fails" for an Architect, it is usually because they are trying to feel instead of design, following someone else's method, or operating in a system that contradicts their blueprint.

Once aligned, results appear quietly and inevitably.

The Architect's Monadic Veto

For Architects, the veto activates when the structure is compromised, integrity is bypassed, or they are asked to hold chaos indefinitely.

This is not avoidance, but a design protection.

Moment of Recognition

If you've spent your life feeling like you see what others don't, you carry systems that others benefit from, and you crave clarity more than comfort.

You are not cold. You are not distant. You are not detached from life. You are architectural.

CHAPTER 9

The Anchor Blueprint

Anchor souls are designed to hold frequency.

Where Architects build systems, Anchors stabilize them. They are not here to redesign reality, disrupt it, or accelerate it. They are here to keep it coherent — emotionally, energetically, and physically.

Anchors are the reason environments don't fracture. Their presence alone changes the field.

Core Orientation

The Anchor blueprint is oriented toward grounding, continuity, emotional regulation, and energetic containment.

Anchors instinctively ask themselves if the situation is safe, if it can be sustained, and what needs to be held steady.

They do not rush. They do not chase. They remain.

Strengths of the Anchor

When Anchors are aligned, they create safety without control, stabilize volatile environments, absorb intensity without collapsing, and provide consistency that others rely on. Because of these strengths, Anchors often become caregivers, healers, community pillars, long-term partners, and quiet leaders.

Their power is subtle but profound. Without Anchors, nothing lasts.

Common Distortions

Anchors are frequently misassigned into roles such as emotional dumping grounds, permanent supporters who receive no support themselves, those who hold together what should end, and individuals who sacrifice themselves for the sake of stability.

This often leads to emotional exhaustion, loss of identity, suppressed resentment, and chronic depletion.

Anchors do not lose themselves suddenly. They erode slowly.

Relationship Patterns

Anchors often attract catalysts who destabilize, architects who forget to rest, and fragmented souls who are seeking safety.

When unconscious, Anchors become containers for others' chaos. When conscious, they choose where and for whom they anchor.

In healthy relationships, Anchors are able to receive as much as they give, step away without guilt, and be steady without being stuck.

Manifestation Style

Anchors manifest through presence, not pursuit.

Their alignment is activated when they feel rooted, when their environment feels coherent, and when their nervous system is respected.

When manifestation stalls, it is usually because they are holding what is not theirs, are anchored to outdated roles, or confuse loyalty with alignment. Once realigned, their life stabilizes quickly and often without dramatic change.

The Anchor's Monadic Veto

For Anchors, the veto activates when stability becomes sacrifice, holding turns into self-erasure, or loyalty overrides truth.

The veto often manifests as a sudden emotional shutdown, physical fatigue, or an inability to continue as before.

This is not a collapse, but a self-preservation.

A Moment of Recognition

If you've spent your life being the calm one, the reliable one, and the one who stays, but you still feel unseen, drained, or taken for granted — you are not weak. You are not passive. You are not meant to disappear into others; you are an Anchor.

CHAPTER 10

The Bridge Soul Blueprint

Bridge souls are designed to translate between worlds.

They move between systems, perspectives, cultures, emotional states, and levels of awareness with unusual ease. Where others choose a side, Bridges naturally hold both — not in confusion, but in comprehension.

They are not here to belong fully to one place.
They are here to connect what would otherwise remain separate.

Core Orientation

The Bridge blueprint is oriented toward translation, integration, mediation, and movement between states.
Bridge souls instinctively ask how two things connect, what is being misunderstood, and what needs to be carried across.

They perceive reality as fluid, layered, and contextual.

Strengths of the Bridge

When aligned, Bridges help systems communicate, reduce conflict through understanding, carry ideas from one realm to another, and make the unfamiliar accessible.

Because of these strengths, Bridges often become mediators, teachers, interpreters, guides, and cross-disciplinary thinkers.

Their gift is not dominance — it is clarity across difference.

Common Distortions

Bridge souls are often misassigned into roles that require permanent loyalty to one side, emotional overextension, constant explanation without rest, and being "the middle" without support.

This often leads to identity diffusion, chronic indecision, emotional fatigue, and a feeling of being unseen by all sides.

Bridges do not break loudly.

They thin.

Relationship Patterns

Bridge souls often attract polarized individuals, conflicted systems, and souls who need help understanding themselves or each other.

When unconscious, Bridges become translators without boundaries.

When conscious, they choose when to cross and when to stay.

In healthy relationships, Bridges can be understood without explaining, rest in one place without guilt, and be whole without being split.

The Bridge's Monadic Veto

For Bridge souls, the veto activates when translation turns into self-erasure, mediation replaces authenticity, or movement is restricted.

The veto may appear as sudden withdrawal, loss of voice, or a refusal to continue explaining.

This is not disengagement, but a boundary restoration.

If you've lived feeling between worlds, too complex for simple labels, and understood but not truly known,

You are not indecisive. You are not fragmented. You are not meant to choose a side; then you are a Bridge.

CHAPTER 11

Chapter 11

The Catalyst Blueprint

Catalyst souls are designed to initiate change. They do not stabilize systems, nor do they translate between systems or build them for longevity. Instead, they activate movement wherever they go, sometimes fostering growth, sometimes causing collapse, and often both. This is not because they are inherently disruptive, but because stagnation cannot survive their presence.

Core Orientation

The Catalyst blueprint is oriented toward activation, transformation, awakening, and breaking inertia. Catalysts instinctively ask questions such as: What is no longer true? What is ready to shift? Where is energy being suppressed? They sense when a system has reached its limit, even if it still appears to function.

Strengths of the Catalyst

When aligned, Catalysts ignite dormant potential, accelerate awareness, initiate necessary endings, and inspire movement without force.

They often become visionaries, change agents, innovators, disruptors, and way-showers.

Their value lies not in what they build, but in what they make possible.

Common Distortions

Catalysts are frequently misassigned into roles that demand consistency over truth, containment of intensity, long-term maintenance, and emotional restraint for the sake of comfort.

This misalignment often leads to restlessness, self-sabotage, burned bridges, and guilt for 'causing disruption.'

Catalysts are often told they are the problem, but they are not; they are the signal.

Relationship Patterns

Catalysts often attract Anchors who try to stabilize them, Architects who want to structure them, and Bridges who try to explain them.

When unconscious, Catalysts leave chaos behind.

When conscious, they initiate with clarity.

Healthy relationships allow Catalysts to be honest without apology, leave without being villainized, and trigger growth without staying to manage it.

Manifestation Style

Catalysts manifest through alignment with timing, not control.

Their life moves in bursts of rapid change, sudden opportunity, and swift endings followed by new openings.

Manifestation stalls when they resist movement, stay where energy is dead, or mistake intensity for instability.

Once aligned, momentum returns immediately.

The Catalyst's Monadic Veto

For Catalysts, the veto activates when stagnation is normalized, truth is silenced, or movement is blocked.

The veto appears as sudden exits, abrupt endings, or a non-negotiable inner command to leave.

This is not recklessness. It is design integrity.

If you've spent your life feeling like a storm that clears the air, unwelcome in stable environments, or responsible for change you didn't intend, you are not destructive, you are not unreliable, and you are not meant to stay. You are a Catalyst.

CHAPTER 12

Misuse of Blueprint Knowledge

Blueprint knowledge is descriptive, not permissive. It explains function. It does not excuse behavior.

When Blueprint Becomes Identity

Problems arise when individuals collapse their Blueprint into personality.

"I am this" becomes justification rather than orientation.

The Blueprint was never meant to replace accountability.

Romanticizing Design

Some individuals glorify their Blueprint.

Intensity becomes virtue. Withdrawal becomes superiority. Control becomes "discernment." This is distortion, not alignment.

Weaponizing the Blueprint

Blueprint language can be used to dominate conversations, invalidate others, or avoid responsibility.

"This is just how I'm designed" becomes a shield against feedback.

Design does not override impact.

Avoidance Disguised as Truth

Unintegrated traits are often reframed as spiritual authority.

Reactivity is mislabeled as honesty. Detachment is mislabeled as wisdom. Instability is mislabeled as evolution. This delays maturation.

Blueprint vs. Conditioning

Blueprints describe how energy moves, not how wounds behave.

Trauma can mimic design traits. Healing clarifies Blueprint expression. Avoidance distorts it.

The Role of Consciousness

A conscious Blueprint refines its function. An unconscious Blueprint repeats patterns. Awareness determines expression, not type.

Monadic Veto Misinterpretation

The Monadic Veto is often misunderstood as impulsive authority.

It is not reactive. It is not emotional. It is not performative.

When used unconsciously, it fractures trust.

Correct Use of Blueprint Knowledge

Blueprint awareness is for self-recognition, appropriate placement, and functional alignment; it is not for justification, comparison, or hierarchy.

Closing Statement

The Blueprint does not absolve. It informs.

Maturity is measured not by knowing your design, but by how responsibly you live it.

CHAPTER 13

After the Blueprint

Once you have seen the structures and recognized the patterns of your journey, the mind naturally asks, 'What do I do now?' The truth is simple: there is nothing left to do. You see, the Blueprint was never a system for you to follow, a role you had to perform, or an identity you had to adopt. If you tried to 'become' the Blueprint, you would actually miss the point entirely.

The Blueprint doesn't activate you; it reminds you. Think of it like a compass placed quietly in your hand, it doesn't shout directions at your mind, it simply orients your soul. You weren't asked to choose this path, but rather to notice where you finally stopped resisting it. That moment when things felt quiet, obvious, and strangely familiar? That was Recognition. And recognition doesn't argue; it settles.

If you find yourself asking, 'How do I live this?' or 'What comes next?', just pause. Those questions come from old conditioning, not from your true alignment. The only shift that actually matters is a quiet one. You might notice you feel less urgency, you need fewer explanations, and there is a sudden reduction in effort.

It isn't dramatic. The Blueprint doesn't create fireworks; it removes friction.

Check in with yourself right now, without over-thinking it:

- Do you feel more still?
- Do you feel less pressure to 'become' something?
- Do you feel oddly unchanged, yet so much clearer?

If the answer is yes, then the Blueprint has landed. You are neither behind nor early. The Blueprint doesn't move forward; it simply waits until you stop running past yourself."

CHAPTER 14

Chapter 14

Living Without Reference

There is a threshold in the journey where you simply stop checking the map. It isn't because you have finally memorized every turn or reached a perfect understanding, but because the deep internal "knowing" has made confirmation unnecessary. You have entered a state of stabilization.

The Mind's Retreat

The human mind is a creature of frameworks, language, and labels. It craves the safety of a "Twin Flame" title or a "Mission" status to feel secure. But the Soul Blueprint doesn't fight the mind; it simply makes its grip irrelevant. What once demanded an exhaustive explanation now moves through you in silence.

You may notice your identity beginning to soften. You speak less about who you are, you explain your motives less to others, and you find you have absolutely nothing left to defend.

Alignment does not perform for an audience. If you find yourself trying to convince someone of your connection, teach the "right" way, or translate your internal experience into 3D words, pause. Truth does not travel through the friction of persuasion; it transmits through the clarity of your presence.

In this space, nothing appears to "change," yet everything is different:

- Decisions take less time because there is no mental static to sift through.
- Emotional hooks loosen, as the need for validation from the outside world dissolves.
- External noise loses its authority over your peace.

This is not an upgrade of your old life; it is a subtraction of everything that wasn't you.

Eventually, even the language of the Blueprint becomes unnecessary. These concepts were merely scaffolding: temporary structures used to support you while your true foundation was being built. Once the structure of your "knowing" stands on its own, the scaffolding is removed.

You are not becoming something new; you are remembering how little was ever required of you. If you feel unfinished, that is as it should be. Completion belongs to stories and narratives, but Blueprints leave space. And it is in that open, quiet space that something finally, deeply rests.

CHAPTER 15

Chapter 15

When Manifestation Stops Trying

There is a moment after the Blueprint is recognized when effort quietly leaves the room. Not because nothing happens, but because nothing needs to be pushed anymore.

Most people believe manifestation is about doing more. More intention. More visualization. More alignment practices stacked on top of exhaustion.

But the Blueprint does not respond to effort. It responds to recognition.

The Misunderstanding

When manifestation fails, people assume:

- they didn't want it badly enough
- they didn't raise their frequency enough
- they didn't heal enough first

But what actually happened was simpler and more precise:

The design did not consent.

113

This is where Monadic Veto becomes visible not as an obstruction, but as intelligence.

Manifestation from a 5D View

From a higher vantage point, manifestation is not creation. It is permissioned emergence.

Things arrive when:

- timing matches design
- form matches function
- identity no longer contradicts outcome

If any of those are misaligned, reality does not punish.
It pauses.

Why Forcing Feels Heavy

Effort feels heavy because it is 3D logic trying to override a multidimensional architecture.

The Blueprint already knows:

- what you can hold
- what you cannot sustain
- what would fracture you even if you "received" it

So when something refuses to arrive, it is not absence.
It is containment.

The Shift That Changes Everything

The moment manifestation begins to work differently is when the question changes.

Not:

"How do I make this happen?"

But:

"What part of me is not designed to carry this yet, or at all?"

That question collapses struggle.

What Happens Next

Once the Blueprint is honored:

- manifestation becomes quiet
- movement becomes obvious
- choices simplify

You stop chasing signs. You stop negotiating with the universe. You stop performing readiness.

And things begin to show up as if they were always scheduled.

A Truth Most Teachings Skip

Some desires are not delayed. They are non-transferable. No amount of belief can override design. No technique can bypass Monadic Veto. And no spiritual maturity changes architecture.

This is not limitation. This is precision.

The Relief No One Talks About

When you finally see your Blueprint clearly, you stop blaming yourself for what never moved.

You realize:

- it wasn't resistance
- it wasn't fear
- it wasn't karma

It was simply not yours to manifest. And what is yours begins to move without force.

CHAPTER 16

The Disorientation Phase

Recognition does not arrive as clarity. It arrives as destabilization.

You expect the Blueprint's unveiling to organize life into purpose and calm. Instead, the familiar anchors dissolve. Identity, once stabilized externally through striving and friction, now turns inward for its root. The external world—goals, roles, validations, loses its grip. What remains is a vast, untethered silence.

Many report the same unraveling: a floating sensation, motivation evaporating like mist, passions fading to neutral gray, a quiet that borders on emptiness. This is not regression. This is decompression. The nervous system, long accustomed to urgency's roar, suddenly hears only its own echo. Silence registers as loss until it reveals itself as space.

Direction once came from friction, from chasing worth, from fixing wounds, from proving existence through motion. When the Monadic Veto activates and overrides misaligned pursuits, those drivers disengage. Adrenaline recedes. Narratives collapse. The familiar struggle that once defined you dissolves. Identity, built on effort and reaction, finds its scaffolding removed. What feels unfinished is, in truth, the first taste of completion.

There is a gap no one names aloud: between the self you performed as the compensatory version armored in hustle and the monadic expression you are designed to be. This gap feels like floating in a void, no wind, no ground. The mind rushes to label it depression, spiritual boredom, or purposelessness. But it is a reorientation in progress. The old compass is dismantled; the new one calibrates in stillness.

Former desires turn hollow not because they were false, but because they were compensatory, manufactured to anchor worth, direction, identity when the Blueprint lay veiled. Once sovereignty reclaims the field, those goals echo like empty costumes. You look upon ambitions that once consumed you and feel... nothing. Neutrality. The fire was borrowed from distortion; now it returns to its source.

In this phase, the false urge to replace the noise surges. People rush to start something new, reinvent themselves, adopt another framework, or anything to fill the pause. This is the mistake. Disorientation does not ask for replacement. It asks for stillness. The system needs time to recalibrate without interference. To rush is to interfere with the monad's quiet directive.

Behind the scenes, unseen currents rebuild: motivation shifts from pressure to resonance; desire purifies itself of compensatory layers; timing awareness reconfigures to the rhythm of essence rather than urgency. This cannot be forced. Orientation returns organically, like dawn after the longest night, no effort required.

Eventually, the subtle click arrives. Decisions feel obvious, not labored. Energy returns selectively, not in frantic bursts. Movement becomes voluntary, not obligatory. You do not "find" your purpose. You stop searching for it. Purpose was never lost; it was obscured by the hunt. When the hunt ends, it reveals itself as the natural expression of what already is.

This in-between feels uncomfortable because pretense is no longer possible. Hustle loses its justification. Misalignment cannot be rationalized. The old games end. But this is also the final phase where confusion reigns. Once orientation stabilizes internally, it does not leave again. The external anchors may dissolve completely, yet the inner compass holds—steady, sovereign, unshakeable.

What to do in this phase is radical in its simplicity:

Observe without judgment. Rest in the floating without apology. Allow desires to die naturally, like leaves releasing from the branch.

What not to do is equally clear:

Do not force clarity through willpower. Do not chase meaning to escape the pause. Do not pathologize the stillness as failure.

This is not emptiness. It is design realigning itself.

When internal identity stabilizes, external anchors dissolve. And in that dissolution, the true orientation begins not as something you chase, but as something you remember you already are.

The Soul Blueprint was never lost. It was only waiting for the noise to quiet so it could speak.

CHAPTER 17

Chapter 17

When Relationships Fracture

As your Soul Blueprint stabilizes, you may notice some relationships begin to change. Not because of fights or big arguments, but quietly. Messages become less frequent. Invitations stop coming. Conversations that used to feel meaningful now feel short and surface-level. The connection doesn't end with drama; it simply fades.

This happens because many relationships were built on practical functions rather than true alignment. They often formed around things like shared ways of handling stress, mutual emotional support that filled a need, matching patterns of insecurity, or similar ways of getting through daily life. These elements created a sense of closeness, but they were compensatory; they helped both people manage discomfort or unmet needs.

When your Blueprint becomes clear and internal stability arrives, those functions become unnecessary. Your system no longer needs the same exchanges to feel okay. There's no more energy to give or receive in the old ways. Without that functional glue, the relationship naturally thins out until only silence remains.

This isn't anyone's fault. No one has to be the bad one. There may still be genuine care, respect, or positive feelings left over. But real connection requires resonance, shared frequency, not just history or habit. When the resonance is gone, keeping the relationship going takes effort. Your system automatically stops making that effort.

You might find yourself no longer repeating explanations, softening what you really think to avoid conflict, or making yourself emotionally available in ways that used to feel required. This change happens on its own, not because you care less, but because compensation is no longer part of your operating system.

People on the other side often notice and comment: "You've changed," "You seem distant," or "I don't know what happened to you." What they're actually feeling is the loss of access to the old version of you—the one who reacted, accommodated, or adjusted to keep things smooth. When those reactions stop, the familiar entry point disappears.

Some relationships simply dissolve quietly. They fade without any need for repair or final conversations. Others shift to a different level: less frequent contact, fewer words, but more direct and honest when it does happen. These connections require almost no explanation, no constant reassurance, and no emotional back-and-forth. They feel open and easy, rather than heavy or managed.

Even when an ending feels right on a deeper level, grief can still show up. You're not necessarily grieving the person themselves. You're grieving the role you used to play in that dynamic—the part of you that adapted, fixed, or performed to keep the connection alive. That version of you is gone, and it's natural to feel the loss of what it represented.

Trying to force explanations or closure usually doesn't work well. Blueprint changes happen inside you first; they're not easy to put into words that someone else can fully understand if they haven't gone through something similar. Explaining your shift often leads to misunderstanding or frustration on both sides. Silence, in this case, isn't avoidance. It's a way of protecting the clarity you've gained.

In some cases, care, respect, and fondness remain even after intimacy, immediacy, and emotional dependency fade. This isn't a downgrade or a failure. It's recalibration— the relationship adjusting to match the new level of alignment (or lack of it).

The people who stay in your life don't ask for your energy, your constant explanations, or the return of your old self. They adapt naturally. Being around them feels neutral and present rather than effortful or performative.

Underneath any sadness, you may start to notice unexpected benefits: a sense of calm you didn't expect, less anxiety about what others think, and a kind of emotional efficiency where feelings move through you more quickly and cleanly. This isn't becoming cold or detached. Its coherence, your inner system runs more smoothly without unnecessary interference.

The basic rule for relationships after Blueprint recognition is straightforward: If it takes ongoing effort to maintain, it's misaligned. If it allows honesty without drama, it belongs.

There's no chasing, no repeated repair cycles, no forced closeness. Just clear truth, when it's there, and space when it isn't.

These fractures aren't signs that something went wrong. They're signs of precision. The Blueprint is removing what no longer fits, so what does fit can emerge, quietly, naturally, and without force. What stays, or what comes later, will feel like recognition rather than work.

CHAPTER 18

Intimacy & Attraction After Blueprint Recognition

Attraction does not disappear after Soul Blueprint recognition. It reorganizes.

What used to draw you in strongly may suddenly feel neutral, confusing, or even out of reach. This shift can be disorienting at first. It doesn't mean desire is gone; it means the old unconscious patterns that fueled attraction are no longer active.

Before Blueprint recognition, attraction was often driven by deeper, less conscious factors. These included nervous system compatibility that created a sense of safety in familiarity, unresolved emotional wounds that mirrored each other, survival patterns that aligned in ways that felt intense, or heightened emotional states mistaken for true chemistry. These bonds could feel electric and compelling, but they were often unstable, built on triggers and compensations rather than steady alignment.

When the Monadic Veto activates and the Blueprint stabilizes, those underlying charges dissolve. Emotional hooks release. Trauma-based polarity collapses. The urgency that once lived in the body fades away. The nervous system stops confusing stimulation or intensity with genuine connection. What remains is clarity: attraction becomes cleaner and more discerning.

You may notice a complete lack of impulse to chase or pursue anyone. There's no fear of losing attention, no anxiety about being chosen or overlooked. The old pattern of "chasing energy" simply stops. If someone needs to be convinced, persuaded, or won over, the bond no longer fits. Attraction no longer pulls you forward; it meets you exactly where you are.

Desire itself becomes more selective. It moves more slowly, quieter, and with greater precision. You're no longer pulled toward potential, what someone could become, or fantasy projections of who they might be. Emotional volatility, once exciting, now feels draining or mismatched. Instead, you're drawn to stability that carries real depth: calm presence, consistency, and resonance without drama.

This change can feel unsettling. People who once triggered longing or excitement may now seem flat, repetitive, or emotionally loud. They haven't necessarily changed; your system no longer interfaces with the old patterns that made them magnetic. The familiar triggers simply don't register anymore.

Blueprint-aligned intimacy doesn't require performance. There's no need for seduction strategies, elaborate emotional disclosure rituals, or constant escalation of intensity to keep things alive. Connection happens naturally without games, without forcing closeness, without the need to prove or earn anything. It feels straightforward and spacious rather than effortful.

These shifts are part of the Blueprint's precision at work. It removes what was compensatory or unconscious, so that what remains is authentic. Attraction and intimacy become expressions of alignment rather than reactions to distortion. What draws you now isn't a fix or a thrill, it's a quiet recognition of shared frequency.

In Blueprint-aligned intimacy, presence replaces performance. Silence no longer feels awkward or tense. Eye contact becomes grounding and steady rather than something that activates old patterns or requires a response. The interaction stays simple and real.

Your body often registers these changes before your mind fully processes them. You may notice relaxed breathing that happens without effort, a steady heart rate even in close moments, and the absence of the usual background anxiety. At first, this calm can feel strange or even boring to a system that was used to emotional charge or intensity for stimulation. But this "boredom" is actually safety deep safety without any dullness or numbness. It's the nervous system finally resting in coherence instead of bracing for the next trigger.

Some people experience a temporary decrease in sexual interest or libido during this phase. This isn't repression or a problem to fix. It's recalibration. Your system is quietly uninstalling old scripts that linked desire to validation, approval, or emotional highs. It's disentangling attraction from past wounds or compensatory needs. It's rebuilding the pathways of desire from a cleaner foundation. When sexuality returns, it does so more authentically, less driven by urgency, more rooted in genuine presence and mutual resonance.

When a Blueprint-compatible attraction does reappear, it feels calm but unmistakable. It's mutual without any need for negotiation or games. It's grounded and steady, without the heavy "gravity" of compulsion or fear. There is no confusion or second-guessing. You don't question the timing, the other person's interest, or their availability. Everything aligns obviously and naturally.

A common fear during the pause or reorganization phase is the worry that you'll "never feel it again," that attraction or passion is permanently gone. This fear is understandable but unfounded. You are not losing attraction itself. You are losing the compulsive, reactive version of it. What remains is true choice: the ability to feel drawn toward someone from a place of wholeness rather than from lack or intensity. When the right resonance arrives, the spark returns. It is clearer, steadier, and without the old drama.

These changes are the Blueprint doing its precise work. It removes what was built on distortion so that intimacy and attraction can express what is real and aligned. What emerges is a connection that feels effortless, honest, and deeply satisfying because it's no longer trying to fill a void.

CHAPTER 19

Twin Dynamics vs Blueprint Alignment

Some people confuse Blueprint alignment with the intensity of soul bonds, especially twin flame or deep karmic connections. The two feel different in the body and in daily life, and recognizing the distinction helps prevent misinterpreting one for the other.

Soul bonds often activate strong memories and emotions from the past. They can feel electric, familiar, or overwhelming. This is because they trigger recognition of shared history, unresolved patterns, or mirrored wounds. The resulting intensity recalls old timelines, pulls up deep feelings, and creates a sense of urgency or destiny. It activates the nervous system in powerful and magnetic ways.

Blueprint alignment, on the other hand, stabilizes presence in the here and now. It brings calm clarity rather than heightened charge. It doesn't pull you back into past stories or forward into dramatic futures; it anchors you in steady awareness. Intensity looks back; alignment builds forward from a grounded place.

Post-Blueprint intimacy redefines itself completely. It is no longer about merging into one another, rescuing or being rescued, or consuming each other's energy to feel whole. Those patterns were compensatory; they filled gaps or soothed wounds. True Blueprint-aligned intimacy is about coexisting as separate, sovereign beings while sharing space. It involves witnessing each other without needing to fix or change anything, and choosing connection from a place of freedom rather than necessity. There is no collapse into oneness, no fusion that blurs boundaries. Just a clear, honest presence.

The new law of attraction after Blueprint recognition is simple and reliable: If something excites the nervous system but leaves you feeling destabilized, off-center, or emotionally drained, it is not alignment. If it calms the system, sharpens your awareness, and leaves you feeling more grounded and present, it is alignment.

This does not mean passion disappears or that life becomes flat. It means passion becomes precise. The old version of passion was often fueled by drama, urgency, or the thrill of uncertainty. The new version arises from stability, mutual recognition, and quiet depth. It feels sustainable rather than consuming, steady rather than explosive.

These shifts are the Blueprint refining what connection can be. It removes what was built on memory or compensation so that what remains is authentic and supportive of your wholeness. You don't lose the capacity for deep intimacy; you gain the ability to experience it without losing yourself.

CHAPTER 20

Chapter 20

Sexuality After Blueprint Recognition

Sexuality does not disappear after Blueprint recognition. It simply changes jurisdiction.

Before recognition, sexuality often operated through validation, polarity wounds, intensity seeking, or nervous system stimulation. These elements made sex feel urgent or necessary. It was frequently used to regulate emotions, feel chosen, anchor identity, or discharge overwhelm. When those underlying needs dissolve with Blueprint alignment, sexuality no longer carries those extra jobs. It becomes honest. That honesty can feel confronting at first because the old motivations are gone.

Many people notice a sexual feeling "in demand" during this transition, not because the desire for sex increases dramatically, but because the old patterns stop working. Attraction reorganizes. Libido detaches from anxiety and compulsion. The system begins asking, "What now?" It wants to understand how desire functions without the previous drivers.

A common experience is a temporary libido dip. Desire may reduce, arousal becomes more selective, and initiation takes longer. This is not a permanent loss or repression. It is the nervous system releasing compulsive loops, detoxing from urgency, and recalibrating its sensation thresholds. When sexuality returns, it does so without begging or forcing. It arises only when conditions align.

Post-Blueprint sexuality no longer chases, proves, or performs. Desire emerges when presence is mutual. If presence is absent, arousal does not occur. If alignment is missing, the system does not override itself. This is the Monadic Veto operating at the level of the body, quietly refusing what no longer fits.

You may notice a lack of interest in dynamics that once felt erotic: power games, push-pull tension, emotional teasing, or intensity escalation. These patterns activated adrenaline, making things feel exciting. Now they register as loud or destabilizing. The body refuses stimulation without safety. Quiet, grounded confidence becomes far more magnetic—not because it tries to be, but because it does not leak energy.

Arousal is now triggered by grounded attention, emotional transparency, energetic stability, and embodied confidence. These qualities feel safe and coherent to the system.

Before alignment, sex often involved fragmentation: part of you was present, part was performing, part was monitoring, or narrating. After Blueprint recognition, the body stays unified. There is no dissociation or mental commentary. Sex becomes fully inhabited.

Awareness increases during this phase, which can make you notice shallow connections, misalignment during touch, or emotional incongruence mid-intimacy. This heightened perception is not judgment; it is the system catching up and protecting wholeness.

When sexuality is Blueprint-compatible, timing feels mutual, initiation happens naturally, and desire flows both ways without bargaining. There is no wondering "Do they want me?" "Am I too much?" or "Should I hold back?" The body already knows the answer.

Pleasure becomes slower, deeper, and less performative. Intensity gives way to depth, and depth lasts longer.

This shift can feel threatening to cultural norms built on scarcity, pursuit, and validation. Blueprint sexuality does not need external approval or seduction; it is sovereign. That sovereignty challenges systems that rely on "seduction economics."

Many people need to hear this clearly: You did not lose desire. You lost tolerance for misalignment.

Sexuality after recognition is no longer a currency, leverage, or something owed. It becomes a shared field rather than a transaction.

The central question changes from "Do they want me?" to "Does my body stay whole here?" If the answer is yes, desire follows naturally. If the answer is no, the system closes gently—no drama, no guilt, just truth.

This is the Blueprint refining sexuality into its most precise and honest expression. What remains is a connection that supports wholeness rather than compensating for anything missing.

CHAPTER 21

Loneliness vs. Solitude After Blueprint Recognition

Loneliness and solitude can feel similar in the body at first. Both are quiet, both remove distractions, both strip away external ways of regulating emotions. But only one is painful.

Blueprint recognition dissolves many habitual connections: unconscious companionship, emotional background noise, and the constant pull of interaction to feel okay. What remains can feel like absence. This isn't because something essential is missing; it's because something false has stopped filling the space. The system is no longer relying on others to manage itself.

Loneliness appears when connection is still anticipated in its old form, but that form is no longer available, and the inner system hasn't fully stabilized yet. It's not simply being alone; it's reaching for something familiar and finding no traction. The mind keeps expecting the old feedback, the old comfort, and when it doesn't arrive, the body registers pain.

Solitude begins when the reaching stops. The system settles. Awareness stays inside the body rather than scanning outward. Nothing is sought, nothing is withheld. The nervous system finally rests because it no longer needs to manage or anticipate anyone else's response.

Many people hit a panic point here. This is where they try to escape the discomfort by re-entering old relationships, lowering their standards, reviving intensity, or confusing familiarity with safety. Blueprint recognition often brings this test, not to punish, but to confirm whether the integration is real. The urge to run back to what's known is strong, but pushing through it allows the shift to complete.

Solitude can feel unnatural at first because identity was previously regulated through interaction, reflection from others, and constant response. Without that external mirror, the mind asks, "Who am I now?" Solitude doesn't answer right away. It creates the space for the answer to form naturally from within.

The quiet can feel "too quiet" at first. This silence is the absence of emotional labor, anticipatory tension, and relational maintenance. For the first time, the system is not managing others or being managed. That absence can feel unsettling before it becomes relieving.

When solitude stabilizes, you may notice clearer thoughts, a slower sense of time, less internal narration, and deeper rest. You stop checking for messages, validation, or cues from others. Nothing is wrong; this is coherence. The body and mind are no longer divided between self and external regulation.

Solitude is not a waiting room for future connection. It is complete in itself. Any connection that arrives later must add to this wholeness, not fill a void.

Loneliness converts into solitude the moment you stop interpreting the silence, stop forecasting negative outcomes, and stop assigning meaning to absence. The system stands on its own—stable, present, and self-contained.

After this shift, being alone no longer aches. Presence no longer collapses without company. Time feels neutral rather than empty. You don't need others to feel real or whole.

Some Blueprints are designed to require more solitude than culture typically allows. This is not withdrawal or avoidance, it's calibration. The system needs low interference, minimal noise, and internal continuity to function at its clearest. Solitude provides exactly that.

Solitude teaches things that cannot be learned through relationships alone: self-trust without external reflection, identity without contrast from others, and worth without a witness. These foundations must form inside first.

When the connection returns, it comes naturally, not urgently or dramatically. It builds on top of solitude rather than replacing it.

The key reframe is simple:

Loneliness says, "I am missing something."
Solitude says, "Nothing is missing."
Both feel quiet. Only one is grounded.

A final truth: If solitude feels stable but unfamiliar, you are
not regressing. You are inhabiting yourself fully for the first
time.

150

CHAPTER 22

Chapter 22

Why Some Relationships Survive Blueprint Shifts
(and Others Don't)

Blueprint recognition does not destroy relationships. It reveals their underlying architecture. Some structures are strong enough to hold under the new conditions. Others collapse quietly, not because of failure, but because they were never designed to support coherence and internal stability.

Before Blueprint recognition, many relationships functioned primarily as forms of regulation: emotional regulators to manage feelings, identity stabilizers to confirm who you were, nervous system anchors to calm anxiety through proximity, or survival mirrors that reflected back familiar patterns. These dynamics worked as long as the system needed external help to feel balanced or safe. When self-regulation arrives through Blueprint alignment, the dependency becomes visible. The relationship no longer needs to serve as a crutch, and that shift exposes what was truly holding it together.

What breaks first are bonds that relied on emotional volatility, mutual wounding, unspoken contracts, or role-based identity. These connections require imbalance or friction to stay alive. They feed on the push-pull, the fixing, or the drama. Blueprint recognition removes the imbalance. Without that fuel, the bond quietly loses energy.

Often, there is no overt conflict. Instead, conversations start to feel flat, effort increases without any real return, and presence simply fades. Nothing dramatic happens— nothing is "wrong," but nothing feels alive anymore. This confuses people because the affection may still be on the surface, yet the connection lacks depth or momentum.

Partners sometimes feel "left behind," but it's not about one person evolving faster than the other. It's that one system has stabilized internally while the other still requires external regulation to function. Stability can feel threatening to a system that bonds through intensity or need; calm presence registers as distance or rejection when what was familiar was a constant emotional exchange.

Relationships that survive share one key feature: they do not rely on fixing, rescuing, or emotional extraction. They are built on mutual sovereignty, two regulated systems that can coexist without needing to manage or be managed. Two unregulated systems can entangle and create intensity. A mixed setup, one stable, one still dependent, tends to struggle because the architectures no longer match.

Love alone is not enough to sustain a relationship after this shift. It must be paired with compatible nervous systems, aligned pacing (similar tolerance for quiet and space), and the ability to be present without constant input. Without these, even genuine affection turns into effort and maintenance.

Blueprint shifts dissolve old roles: caretaker, stabilizer, motivator, emotional container. If the relationship was organized around one person filling a role for the other, it destabilizes. If it were organized around mutual presence rather than roles, it would adapt and expand.

Trying harder, "working on it," stops working because effort cannot repair a structural mismatch. Pushing to fix or revive often accelerates the collapse by highlighting the incompatibility even more clearly. Blueprint recognition removes the illusion that more effort equals true alignment.

Relationships that adapt allow space without punishment. They do not demand emotional labor, panic at silence, or interpret calm as disinterest. They expand rather than tighten, giving each person room to be fully themselves without needing to adjust or perform.

Some relationships end not in conflict, but in completion. There is no villain, no betrayal, no dramatic reason, just incompatibility revealed. This is not abandonment. It is accuracy. Even clean endings carry grief, not for the person necessarily, but for the version of self that needed that bond to feel whole. That grief passes, and clarity remains.

What survives Blueprint recognition is honesty without urgency, presence without performance, and connection without extraction. Anything built on something else quietly exits.

A difficult truth: Some relationships only exist before coherence. They serve as bridges, not destinations. They help carry you to a certain point, then naturally complete their purpose.

The new standard becomes simple: The question is no longer "Can we make this work?" It becomes "Can we remain ourselves here?" If the answer is no, design cannot be overridden by love alone.

Relationships do not fail after Blueprint recognition. They are revealed. And what remains is lighter, cleaner, and real.

CHAPTER 23

Partnership Without Self-Abandonment

Partnership after Blueprint recognition is not primarily about closeness or togetherness. It is about the continuity of the self. If a relationship requires you to shrink, adapt, explain your existence, or override your inner system, it is not aligned, no matter how loving or familiar it feels on the surface.

Before Blueprint recognition, self-abandonment was often normalized in relationships. A compromise happened without real consent; emotional translation was expected to keep the peace; constant self-monitoring was needed to avoid conflict; and identity was softened to fit the dynamic. These patterns were mistaken for love or maturity. In reality, they were survival strategies, ways to maintain connection when inner stability was not yet available.

Blueprint alignment removes the need to bend. The system now refuses distortion automatically. The body reacts immediately to misalignment through tension, fatigue, or a clear internal "no." Effort that once felt like bonding now registers as draining. This is not rigidity or coldness. It is integrity: the Blueprint protecting wholeness.

Many people carry the old fear: "If I don't adapt, I'll be alone forever." But adaptation was never a true connection; it was compliance. When the fear arises, it is the last echo of an unregulated system. The truth is that refusing to abandon yourself does not guarantee loneliness; it guarantees authenticity. What cannot meet you in that authenticity was never meant to stay.

Post-Blueprint partnership requires two regulated nervous systems, mutual respect for each person's pacing, space without punishment, and silence without interpretation. No one manages the other's emotions or energy. Boundaries are no longer negotiated or defended; they are biological limits. You notice when they are crossed and respond accordingly, without apology or lengthy explanation.

Emotional responsibility becomes fully individual. You are no longer responsible for managing someone else's reactions, buffering their discomfort, or maintaining harmony at your own expense. Each partner regulates itself. This makes the connection cleaner and less exhausting.

Some people describe this new way of relating as "cold" because they confuse intensity with intimacy, reactivity with passion, and fusion with closeness. Blueprint partnership feels calmer. Calm is often mistaken for absence or disinterest until it is lived and the depth beneath it becomes clear.

Partnership no longer requires constant togetherness, shared identity, or emotional syncing. It allows two parallel lives to intersect naturally. Autonomy strengthens attraction rather than threatening it. No one disappears into the relationship.

Conflict changes shape. It is no longer emotional escalation, defensive looping, or resolution through exhaustion. It becomes brief, factual, and contained. Repair happens without collapse or lingering resentment because neither person is abandoning themselves to "fix" the moment.

Sacrifice is not love. Blueprint partnership does not ask you to override intuition, tolerate misalignment, or shrink your truth. Real love does not require self-loss.

The difference is subtle but absolute: Before alignment, the feeling was "I need you to feel whole." After alignment, it becomes "I choose you while remaining whole." Need collapses under pressure. Choice holds steady.

This form of partnership feels rare because most relationships are still built on mutual regulation, unconscious contracts, and emotional labor exchange. Blueprint partnership removes all three. What remains is simple and uncommon.

When it works, presence deepens, attraction stabilizes, and individuality remains fully intact. No one disappears. No one manages.

The new measure of love is no longer "How much am I willing to give?" It becomes "Can I stay myself here?" If the answer is yes, the partnership thrives. If the answer is no, clarity replaces attachment.

Blueprint partnership does not demand more of you. It demands nothing you are not. That is its strength.

CHAPTER 24

Love Without Urgency

Urgency was never passion. It was insecurity in motion. Love without urgency does not rush, chase, or grip. It unfolds at the pace of truth, steady and unforced.

Before Blueprint recognition, urgency often felt necessary because it came from fear of loss, fear of missing the "right" timing, fear of not being chosen, or fear of silence. Movement was mistaken for momentum. The faster things progressed, the safer they seemed. Slowing down felt like a risk.

After Blueprint recognition, the system no longer panics. Time stops feeling like an enemy. Silence no longer registers as rejection. Distance does not trigger endless imagination or worst-case scenarios. Nothing is being lost because nothing was ever owned. The nervous system rests in the present rather than bracing for future threats.

Love no longer needs proof to exist. There is no pressure to define the relationship quickly, escalate intimacy to secure it, or clarify feelings repeatedly. Clarity emerges naturally. If it is present, it is felt without words. If it is not, no amount of effort can manufacture it.

You stop asking, "Is this happening fast enough?" Timing is no longer something to manage. Alignment does not expire or run out. What is true does not need acceleration to survive.

This is patience without waiting. Waiting implies expectation and attachment to a specific outcome. Here, there is availability without clinging. Life continues fully. Presence remains steady. You are not paused or on hold; you are simply open.

Desire exists without tension. There is space to want without reaching, to enjoy without securing, to connect without binding. Nothing feels at risk because the foundation is internal rather than dependent on the other person's response.

At first, this can feel unromantic. Romance was often built on urgency, pursuit, and uncertainty, the chase, the drama, the intensity of not knowing. Remove those elements, and what remains feels quiet. Quiet is not absence or boredom. It is stability. The heart no longer races to prove something; it rests in what already is.

Blueprint-aligned love does not escalate to stay alive. It deepens without effort. No milestones, forced progression, or deadlines are needed to justify its existence. It grows through consistency rather than crisis.

Time becomes an ally instead of a test. It stabilizes what is real, clarifies what is unclear, and naturally filters out what does not match. Anything misaligned exits without drama. Anything aligned strengthens quietly over time.

There is no fear of loss because loss requires attachment to a specific outcome. Blueprint love is attached to presence, not possession. If it stays, it stays clean. If it leaves, it leaves clean. Either way, wholeness remains intact.

Trust shifts completely. It is no longer a matter of trust in the other person's behavior, promises, or consistency. It is trust in design: if it fits the Blueprint, it holds naturally. If it does not, it dissolves naturally. No forcing, no clinging.

Love becomes recognition rather than acquisition. You do not gain it or conquer it. You recognize it. There is no conquest, no securing, no earning. Just resonance meeting resonance.

The final reframe is simple: Love without urgency is not passive. It is settled. Nothing is missing. Nothing is chased. Love stands where it is—steady, clear, and unmistakable.

When urgency leaves, love does not fade. It becomes unmistakable.

CHAPTER 25

Embodying Blueprint Love

Blueprint Love is not something you practice or perform. It is something you inhabit. You don't maintain it, protect it, or work to keep it alive. You simply live from it.

Understanding Blueprint Love intellectually is important, but it is not enough. Without embodiment, insight remains cognitive, something you know in your mind but lose under stress. Old reflexes return, relationships revert to familiar patterns, and coherence slips away when pressure appears. Embodiment is what anchors the Blueprint under real-life conditions. It keeps the system stable when life tests it.

Embodiment begins in the body. Blueprint Love lives in regulated breath that stays even, grounded posture that feels rooted, unhurried movement that carries no rush, and steady eye contact that conveys presence without demand. The body signals safety and coherence before any words are spoken. Others feel this steadiness instinctively, even if they cannot name it.

You no longer translate yourself for others. Over-explaining feelings, justifying boundaries, or softening the truth to make it palatable stops automatically. Your system speaks clearly without needing volume or repetition. The message is carried in your presence, not in endless clarification.

Relational monitoring ends. You stop checking tone for hidden meaning, tracking responses for approval, or anticipating reactions to avoid conflict. Blueprint embodiment keeps you present rather than vigilant. You are here, fully, without scanning for threats to the connection.

Choice replaces strategy. You don't plan how to relate or script interactions. You simply notice what feels open in your body, what feels closed, and what holds coherence. Then you choose accordingly, staying when it aligns, stepping back when it does not. There is no calculation, only an honest response.

Boundaries become embodied rather than verbal. They are felt as biological limits, not rules to negotiate. When alignment drops, you leave physically or energetically without confrontation. When it holds, you stay. The body knows before the mind needs to decide.

Blueprint Love shows up in daily life through small, consistent ways: how you listen without interrupting to fix, how you pause before responding, how you meet silence without filling it, how you don't rush connection to feel secure. Love is no longer an event or a special moment. It becomes a steady state that runs underneath everything.

In conflict, the body is no longer hijacked. You may still feel sensation, heat, or activation, but you do not abandon yourself to manage the other person's experience. Presence stays intact. You remain regulated even when the moment is uncomfortable.

Sexuality becomes an extension of embodiment. Desire responds to authenticity, steadiness, and mutual presence, not to performance, seduction, or escape. It arises from wholeness rather than need.

Embodiment makes you unmistakable. You stop being ambiguous, energetically available to misalignment, or readable through old patterns. People feel where you stand without explanation. Your field is clear and consistent.

Blueprint Love lasts because nothing is suppressed, nothing is forced, and nothing is pursued. It doesn't need external momentum to survive. It has its own gravity—quiet, steady, and self-sustaining.

Embodiment is not perfection. You will still feel emotion, experience fluctuation, and need space at times. The difference is that you no longer disconnect from yourself to stay connected to another. Wholeness remains the baseline.

The quiet proof of Blueprint Love is simple: You feel more yourself in connection than you do when alone, not less. The presence of another amplifies rather than diminishes who you are.

Blueprint Love is not a relationship style or technique. It is a state of being in relationship with yourself first, and then with another. Once embodied, it cannot be unlearned. It becomes the new default.

CHAPTER 26

Living Blueprint Love in Everyday Life

When the Blueprint fully integrates, it ceases to be a destination and becomes the very ground you walk upon. We often mistake "Love" for a feeling we enter or a romance we pursue, but Blueprint Love is far more vast. It is an organizing force that reshapes everything from the way you wake in the morning to the way you leave a room.

The End of Self-Correction

For a long time, you may have felt like your life was a series of constant adjustments, fine-tuning your tone, managing your energy, or calculating the perfect timing for your actions. In the presence of the Blueprint, this editing simply stops. You begin to move as one whole piece. You no longer explain yourself because you are no longer trying to "fit" into a frequency that isn't yours.

The Simplicity of Action

In this state, decision-making loses its weight. You no longer need to debate or justify your choices to the world. There is only one question that remains: "Does this keep me whole?".

- If yes: You proceed.

- If no: You decline.

This clarity extends into your work and how you contribute to the world's energy. You stop working for approval, recognition, or positioning. Instead, you work from a place of pure transparency. Paradoxically, as your output becomes cleaner, it becomes more impactful. You are no longer "trying" to make a difference; your existence is the difference.

Energetic Efficiency

Your social world will naturally recalibrate to match this internal shift. You may notice fewer interactions, but the ones that remain are significantly deeper. Your tolerance for "noise" disappears, and you find yourself making quicker exits from spaces that do not resonate—doing so without a trace of guilt. This is not a withdrawal from the world; it is energetic efficiency.

The New Rhythm of Time

Time itself begins to feel different. The pressure to "keep up" or the fear of being "behind" vanishes. You stop rushing because you realize the Blueprint does not move forward; it waits for you to inhabit the life you already have. Love is no longer a room you walk into; it is the tone you carry with you into every moment.

Blueprint Recognition

- Unedited Movement: Do you feel less pressure to "fix" your presentation for others?

- Instant Decisiveness: Are your "yes" and "no" becoming effortless and quiet?

- Impact through Clarity: Is your work feeling more effective because you've stopped seeking approval for it?

CHAPTER 27

Creation, Service, and Contribution from Coherence

When you live from the Blueprint, your work in the world undergoes a radical transformation. For a long time, you may have believed that "helping" meant fixing, rescuing, or proving your value to others. You worked from a place of urgency, often pushing your energy until you reached the point of burnout.

But in the state of Coherence, the need to "try" to help disappears. You realize that your greatest contribution is not what you do, but the clarity you carry.

Precision in Creation

Your creative energy becomes precise. You find yourself creating less, perhaps moving slower, but acting with far more intention. Because you are no longer performing for an audience or seeking approval, every word you speak and every action you take carries weight. There is no more "filler" in your life—only resonance.

Leadership Without Force

True leadership in the Blueprint does not require persuasion. You don't need to convince anyone to follow you or believe in your vision. Instead, people respond to you because you are steady. Your mere presence organizes the space around you, acting like a tuning fork that helps others find their own frequency.

Service Without Burnout

Burnout is a symptom of self-abandonment; it happens when you give from a place of obligation rather than from a place of overflow. The Blueprint ends this cycle. You no longer pursue connections or results. You simply allow resonance to happen. Those who are meant to engage with your energy will do so, and those who aren't, won't. There is no pursuit, only alignment.

Blueprint Recognition

- From Urgency to Alignment: Does your work feel like an overflow rather than a chore?
- Ending the Rescue Mission: Have you stopped trying to "fix" others and started focusing on your own clarity?
- The Weight of Presence: Do you notice that you can influence a room just by being still and steady within it?

CHAPTER 28

Closing the Book Without Closing the Path

As you reach these final words, understand that this book was never intended to be an initiation. It was a recognition. There are no complex exercises to follow, no integration plans to map out, and no further steps to take. If the truth within these pages resonated with you, then it has already integrated into your frequency.

There is No Practice

We often believe that spiritual growth requires constant effort, but the Blueprint operates differently. You are not "becoming" a new version of yourself; you are simply remembering the original structure of your soul. Blueprint Love was never something you had to learn; it was something waiting to be uncovered.

The Only Metric That Matters

As you move back into the world, notice the subtle shifts in your reality.

- If life feels quieter: That is not a loss; it is the sound of interference leaving your field.
- If relationships shift: That is not a failure; it is a movement toward accuracy.
- If you feel more like yourself: That is the only metric that has ever mattered.

Final Release

You do not need to hold onto this book, quote its lines, or even agree with its concepts. If its frequency matched yours, it will stay with you. If it didn't, it will simply pass through.

The Landing

You are not behind. You are not early. You are not missing anything. The Blueprint does not move forward. It waits... until you stop running past yourself.

Blueprint Love is not the future. It is what remains when nothing false is required to stay.

- Recognition over Choice: Did you stop "trying" and start noticing where you already fit?
- End of Seeking: Has the need for labels and constant explanations finally loosened its grip?
- The Space of Rest: Do you feel the "quiet recognition" that nothing more is required?

CHAPTER 29

Chapter 29

Blueprint Love

I didn't set out to define a new kind of love.

While writing this book, I realized that what I was experiencing could no longer fit inside the meaning of unconditional love as the 3D world describes it.

Unconditional love, as I had learned it, often meant endurance. Staying. Forgiving without truth. Giving without self. Loving in ways that quietly asked me to disappear.

What I was living felt different. Stronger. Clearer. Calmer.

It didn't ask me to sacrifice myself in order to love. It didn't require suffering to prove devotion. It didn't need to be validated, chosen, or confirmed.

This love continued without judgment. Without attachment to outcome. Without needing permission.

And that was when I understood something important. Blueprint Love does not come from emotion. It comes from consciousness.

Emotion can be present, but it is not the source. The source is awareness of self, of truth, of alignment.

This kind of love knows where it begins and where it does not cross. It does not collapse into the other. It does not abandon the self to maintain connection.

It simply is.

At first, I wondered about Monadic Veto.

I had come to understand it as protection — a soul-level boundary that prevents distortion. I questioned whether it would interfere with love at this depth.

But it didn't.

Monadic Veto didn't stop me.

It didn't shut my heart down. It didn't interrupt the connection. It didn't block the flow. And that was the confirmation.

Because Monadic Veto does not oppose love. It only activates when love asks you to abandon yourself.

This love never did.

That's how I knew it was aligned with my soul's original design.

Blueprint Love is stronger than unconditional love because it includes the self. There is no hierarchy between loving another and loving oneself. Both are held simultaneously, without conflict.

This is love without collapse. Connection without loss of self. Devotion without distortion.

Blueprint Love is not something we fall into. It is something we become capable of holding.

And as I wrote these words, I realized that this book had been tracing that arc all along from Monadic Veto to Soul Blueprint to conscious connection.

From boundary to coherence to love that knows itself.

And that, I understood, was the love I had been remembering all along.

CHAPTER 30

Chapter 30

Blueprint Love vs. Unconditional Love

Unconditional love is one of the most misunderstood teachings in the 3D world.

It is often presented as the highest form of love — love without limits, without conditions, without boundaries. But in practice, it frequently becomes something else.

Endurance. Tolerance. Staying when truth asks us to leave.

Many people learn unconditional love as a requirement to accept pain, imbalance, or self-erasure in the name of devotion. It is taught as virtue to keep loving even when the soul contracts.

Blueprint Love does not work this way.

Blueprint Love is stronger than unconditional love because it does not require the abandonment of self. It does not ask one to suffer in order to prove depth or loyalty.

Unconditional love often focuses on the other. Blueprint Love holds both.

In Blueprint Love, love flows from consciousness rather than emotion. Because it is conscious, it remains stable. It does not cling. It does not collapse. It does not confuse intensity with truth.

This love does not need to be chosen. It does not need reassurance. It does not seek validation.

It exists without judgment not because anything is allowed, but because clarity is present.

Monadic Veto plays an essential role here.

Contrary to how it is often perceived, Monadic Veto does not block love. It blocks distortion. It only activates when a connection asks the soul to step out of alignment with itself.

That is why Monadic Veto remains silent in Blueprint Love.

There is nothing to veto when love does not require sacrifice.

Blueprint Love allows distance without disconnection. Truth without punishment. Freedom without loss.

This is not love as attachment. It is love as coherence.

When love is aligned with the soul's original design, it does not drain. It does not demand. It does not distort identity.

It simply remains.

EPILOGUE

Epilogue

Like every book I have written, I never truly knew where this one would lead, or how it would end. I did not control the structure, the pacing, or even the words themselves. I only knew that I had to begin.

Once I did, something else took over.

I am not the author in the traditional sense. I am the vessel. The moment I sit down to write, the writing starts writing itself. Thought gives way to listening. Intention dissolves into movement. And what appears on the page feels less like creation and more like remembrance.

The Magic of the Soul Blueprint became yet another confirmation that consciousness is not abstract or distant. It is alive. It thinks, feels, organizes, and experiences itself— sometimes through people, sometimes through love, and sometimes through writing.

This book was not planned. It unfolded. It did not seek an ending. It arrived at one.

And perhaps that is the quiet truth beneath all of it: when consciousness wants to speak, all it needs is a willing hand.

Consciousness didn't split because it lacked something. It split because experience requires perspective.

In unity, love is. In duality, love can be felt.

Consciousness leans into form, into time, into two points of view not to suffer, not to search, but to touch itself from opposite sides.

Blueprint Love in 3D isn't about reunion as an event. It's about recognition as a sensation:

- a glance that feels familiar
- a presence that feels like home
- a calm that doesn't need proof

Two bodies, two nervous systems, two stories carrying the same underlying design. Not halves trying to become whole. But wholeness chooses to experience intimacy. Nothing was ever lost in the split. Wholeness did not break. It only shifted perspective.

Consciousness did not divide because it was incomplete, but because experience requires vantage points. Everything remained intact: the love, the knowing, the blueprint itself. What changed was only where it was being felt from.

Blueprint Love was never about reunion. It was about intimacy, wholeness, choosing to experience itself in form.

And in that realization, I understood:

there was nothing to recover, nothing to fix, and nothing missing at all.

GLOSSARY

Glossary

Monadic Veto

A soul-level boundary that prevents distortion, false merging, or forced timelines. Operates beyond personality or will.

Soul Blueprint

The original energetic design through which a soul experiences incarnation, perception, and manifestation.

Catalyst Blueprint

A soul design that initiates activation, change, or awakening in others, often without personal intention.

Blueprint Love

A form of connection that aligns with the soul's original design rather than emotional dependency, projection, or karmic bonding.

Twin Flame

Two incarnations expressing a single soul blueprint, activating recognition, remembrance, and integration rather than completion.

Embodiment

The process of living soul-level knowing through the body, nervous system, and daily life.

3D / 5D

Reference points for perceptual orientation. 3D emphasizes linear time and separation; 5D emphasizes coherence, resonance, and non-linear awareness.

Manifestation

The natural outcome of alignment between soul blueprint, perception, and action—rather than effort or desire.

Council

A non-physical collective associated with guidance, oversight, or memory beyond a single lifetime.

Coherence

A state of inner alignment where the heart, mind, body, and soul operate as a single, unified field. In coherence, there is no internal conflict or fragmentation; the frequency remains steady regardless of external circumstances. This state allows the Soul Blueprint to express itself naturally in the physical world, without force, effort, or resistance. Coherence is not something achieved; it is something remembered.

Coherence (con't)

The natural harmony that occurs when consciousness is no longer split between fear and truth. In coherence, the soul's frequency stabilizes, allowing manifestation and connection to unfold without distortion. It is the condition that makes Blueprint Love possible in 3D reality.